Faith 401:
Faith Cultivated Love

ISBN: 978-1-944901-32-5

Copyright © 2025 by Speaking Freedom LLC
All rights reserved.
No portion of this book may be reproduced without written permission from the publisher or author, except as permitted by U.S. copyright law.

Book Cover by: Kaci Winslow

Publisher Website: speakingfreedom.org

Other Website Information:
SpeakingfreedomTV.org, edu-freedom.org

Publisher Address: 75 Washington St. #1177, Fairburn, GA 30213

Speaking Freedom Book's Disclaimers

Welcome to Faith 401: Faith Cultivated Love

We thank you for your purchase and we look forward to helping you grow in all areas of your life.

We hope that you find all the information needed for your growth. God bless. Please listen to all disclaimers provided.

If you are currently under physician's care, please maintain that relationship. This audiobook is not intended to stop your current treatment plan. If you need physician's care, please seek out medical attention.

Please note all results are based on the individual's ability to adapt and adjust to any given environment or situation. We are not responsible for your results. The life enhancement coaches at Speaking Freedom provide information to help you grow.

You are responsible for maintaining that growth, taking on and then applying the information to your individual life as you deem needed and necessary. This book was written by Speaking Freedom Books.

For best results, you will need an open mind, the ability to research, and a balanced lifestyle.

Section 1: Introduction

Setting your intentions. While reading this book, I want you to set your intentions, meaning get your mind on something that's truly your heart's desires. Now because this book is specifically about faith cultivated love, I want you to begin to identify the barriers within yourself that keeps you from cultivating the love within to its highest level.

Anything that may present a barrier to loving someone else and allowing someone else in to love you the way that you love you. With each section, I want you to take time to review what you've heard and how you can apply it to your life to help you cultivate your love based on your faith. When setting your intentions, we want you to begin to understand what it will take to manifest the love that your heart truly desires.

Your mindset and overall goal should be, "how will I learn to build healthier relationships with my family, work-related friendships, and romantic partnerships based in love." It's important to know that love and faith are going to bring your strongest types of relationships. When setting your intentions, focus on the type of love you would like to manifest and the things that you can apply from each section in order to help that process.

This can consist of you making a list of the qualities that you enjoy, the things that you like, the qualities that you're looking forward to, the things that you dislike, the things that you don't want, and the things that are relationship breaking points. Every relationship should actually have the same foundational structure. If you are one way with all of your friends, then those friendships can have the ability to grow into business partnerships, romantic relationships, or family-bonded type of friendships.

However, you do need to know the things that you value in relationship, in business, and in partnership to set your intentions properly while manifesting the things that you truly wholeheartedly deeply desire. At the end of each section, you will find a place for reflection and questions. In this particular book, we're going to have you to reflect more on what you've heard than what questions we would like to ask you.

Journal Thoughts

There are going to be some questions, but there will be more reflective points in this book. Your first question is below.

What do you believe is:
Your ideal relationship?
Your ideal friendship?
Your ideal business partnership?
Your romantic relationship?

Write all of those things down and consider, what type of relationships would I like to establish with faith?

Section 2: Love is your Lifeline

By the end of this section you should have a better understanding of your attractions, your selection process, and what it is that you need versus what you think you want. First we're going to learn how and why you are drawn to certain things as well as how that plays into your purpose. What feels like love for you? What draws you into love? Sometimes we are drawn into love by the outer attraction.

Maybe the person looks good, maybe they smell good, maybe they dress nice, maybe they drive something nice, or live in a certain place and it intrigues your mind just based on the surface level things. However, it is very important to see beyond the surface level things, to have an understanding and a concept of exactly what you are selecting and why.

It's okay for everybody to want something different in life. Nobody wants the same exact things because nobody's purpose, interests or perspectives are exactly the same.

This gives us the freedom to be able to pick, choose and select who we are with based on what's a priority and what's important to us in our lives. What feels like love to you? What is your perception of the love given? What makes you feel secure in a relationship? Security for some people comes through financial gain, having material possessions and a place to stay.

When you're thinking of love, "The Maturity Factor" of love allows you to grow beyond the surface level things. The maturity factor of love mixed with faith allows you to see based on what's in the heart of a person to understand their actions. When you begin to uncover the heart of the person, you can see what their priorities are, what's important to them and how they handle priorities.

So one of the best ways to determine what feels like love and how we experience love is by first loving and dating ourselves. I know in previous books, we talked about loving yourself, but this is the other side of loving yourself. Because once you begin to love yourself, date yourself and take yourself seriously, you begin to learn what exactly makes you feel warm, bubbly and giggly inside, especially when it comes to relationships.

Most people experience love differently, depending on how you learned love will determine what you believe love is. Let's start by saying love is not abusive verbally, physically, mentally, financially, or any other way where a person uses something in order to manipulate a situation or suffocate your love in any way. So, why are you drawn to the things that you like? The answer will play into how you learned to love over the years and how you matured in your life.

The second thing to understand is what exactly are you looking for in terms of love? What would you determine love to be for you? What does love look like for you? As I've stated this is a reflective book because a lot of what love is to you is based on what you've learned love to be. You are responsible to reshape what you know about love to fit your purpose in such a way that allows you to grow, evolve and to cultivate love based on the type of faith you have overall, not just faith about love, but faith in every area. You have to apply faith to each portion of your life in order to get the fullness out of it.

Learning why we draw certain things in is essential for getting the results your heart desires. What is it that attracts us and why? Is it something that we can relate to, been through, or healed from? Because the first thing that you have to do is make sure that you are not drawn to or attracting people based off of trauma. If you develop love based off of trauma, and decide or try to heal, then the love would diminish unless you're growing and healing together.

You should've identified your purpose and started to move in the direction of your purpose. This person that you're seeking love from, for, and with, especially when manifesting, should be equal on the opposite side. That means that they have developed their purpose, love themselves so that they know what they want and are healed. When you meet, you're both coming together from a "whole" standpoint within your heart. When you tie in soul purpose, then all you're waiting for is the proper alignment with time for the actual connection because the goal is to manifest your love based on your faith.

To do that, you have to begin to understand the type of love that you need so that you can attract those things by becoming what you need. You are probably wondering, how does the type of love that you desire play into your purpose? How should it feed your soul on top of your individual wholeness? This helps you to determine what you desire most. Do you desire a faith-based love most? Love based off of compassion, trust, and other elements of love itself. Do you want love based totally on friendship? Or do you want a commitment-based love? Really think about this because you need to get a description of the type of love that you want.

If you want full and whole love completely across the board, then you have to determine what would love be for you? What do you think love looks and feels like? What experiences of love have you had to build on?

Sometimes you have to build on your knowledge of love in order to understand what you really desire and how you desire to truly be loved, because love comes in a plethora of ways. Your love could be based on the faith that you have that brings you together in order to move forward.

It can just be based off of the lovey-dovey love or it can be grounded in friendship and commitment so that you understand and respect each other. This helps when you come together beyond the friendship level and you begin to make the bond or commit to a relationship. You have full knowledge, understanding, and comprehension of what you both expect when you get ready to take the step into marriage and commitment based on love. The goal is to manifest this love, to recharge and re-energize love if you are married and or in a committed relationship of any kind. It is important to know that love has many ways to speak.

There are languages of love that communicate how we feel and give love. You have to understand if you are a person that likes gifts, if you are a person that likes affection, communication, acts of service, or kind gestures. What's love to you? For some people, love is getting your spouse or significant other wings or their favorite food as a gesture of love.

Not saying to go and make your significant other gain excessive weight or have them eating unhealthy on a regular basis that have a long-term health effect. However, we are acknowledging that some people like to be dined and being fed spiritually also makes them feel loved. It makes them feel like you care about their well-being because in order to love you have to care about what makes them feel important, feel special, what makes them dance like when your food arrives in a restaurant.

Those are things that we are looking for when we talk about love. Define what your soul desires deeply about love.

What is it about when you see love? A lot of people make couple goals and a lot of people base those goals off of pictures and things that could be a facade or an illusion of sorts. What do you base love on? What are some of your relationship goals personally? Base it on love that you've experienced in person, not based on what you see other people posting online. So it may not be just off of your romantic relationships.

If you know people that have healthy, successful, well-balanced relationships, then the goal is to look at them as examples and see what you like from those examples of real love, insight, and experience. Observe how they get along, overcome challenges, endure things together, and grow stronger and closer. Recognize that not all relationships, have a strong bond when it comes to problem solving, solutions, compromise and really making love last. When I talk about the languages of love, it is very important that you understand the difference between the recipient's language of love and the giver's language of love, knowing how each one desires to be loved and receive love also.

If I am giving you love in a way that is not your love language, then your perception of what I'm doing may not be the love that's intended to be shown when I'm giving whatever language I know. Consider one of the key factors in finding someone is that aligning with those that find it easy to understand your particular love language; so that you're not struggling in the course of your relationship trying to interpret what's meant to be understood easily. When you are always trying to interpret through a different means because they don't understand what makes you feel loved, what makes you tick, feel special, feels like compassion to you, for you, with you, because through that you will be giving the same to the other person. I cannot tell you or define for you what love is to you.

Love is something that's defined from within. Love is something that's connected directly to your purpose because that's how you feel love. That purpose will connect you directly to what love should feel like because it goes hand in hand with your lifestyle choices, your mentality, and decision-making process. What you should desire in a person should play into who you are and what your purpose is. Determining for yourself what makes you feel love is going to be the starting point.

Understand your past decisions in love, like figure out based on your relationships in the last five to ten years. So if in the last 10 years you have not had many close connections or relationships, then consider the last 15 years. What patterns do you see or find in the last relationships that you've had? Again, we don't want to enter relationships based on trauma, hurt, or things that when we heal and as we grow are no longer the things that connect us.

So we disconnect as we proceed to pursue purpose. So generally speaking, love is honor. For example, a person that honors you or somebody that you can honor with your life and decision making.

Love is also value. That means that you value yourself and the person that you're with and they value themselves and you in such a way that it's reflective in their lifestyle choices, the things that they desire and how they think. That person should also hold you in high regards.

That means that they consider you in all things. They understand how you think, respect your mind and the decisions that they're making that will affect your life in any way, shape, form, or fashion. They'll respect you as a person, how you think, how you move, and align with your beliefs and you will be able to honor each other through that respect.

You also need somebody that cares about your goals and your well-being. This goes back to the purpose because if you have a certain set of goals and this can work several different ways because you can have goals that they fund the goals, give into the goals, but if they don't have any interest in your goals, then they won't help you reach your goals in a way that you feel loved and supported. Caring about your well-being is a part of helping you with your goals because your mental, physical, spiritual, and your financial well-being are all important.

The person that you decide to be with should be able to cover you and help you sustain yourself mentally, spiritually, physically, financially. They should want to see you in a better place. It doesn't matter how good you are, you can be a millionaire, a real estate guru, an author, an entrepreneur, you could be an artist of any kind, your partner and friends should want you to go and grow higher.

The love that's for you will meet you wherever you are and grow you wherever you are, not the person but the experience of sharing your love with the person. what does love feel like? What is your perception of love? Sometimes we start out with the wrong perception of what love is and what it should feel like. These questions allow you to examine your beliefs about Love.

For some people, they think love hurts, comes with sorrow and emotional turmoil. Some people have learned that love is dysfunctional, arguing, fighting, and other things that can break a person's spirit. When love is actually what builds your spirit, love is like water to the soul, and your soul needs to be refreshed and replenished on a regular basis, like your body.

So, are you happy with the type of people that you've dated in the past? What are the relationships that has had the biggest positive impact on your life? And why? What about those relationships stand out the most? What relationships have allowed you or caused you to struggle in the past (whether it was financially, mentally, spiritually, or physically)? What was the underlying issue of your failed relationships? What were the things that could have been better? What part did you play in each scenario?

A part of this is going to be in the next section because there has to be a sense of accountability in each and every relationship. This particular section is about dealing with your selection process because some of the things that we endure in relationships that's hard is simply a result of picking someone that we already know is questionable. When we choose someone that already doesn't align with the goals and the things that we believe in, thrive, and strive for, we set ourselves up for tough lessons. When you seek to be in a relationship with someone that doesn't truly align with your heart's desires, then you're seeking dysfunction in the future regardless if it's long term with commitment or a short-term relationship.

Unless you can come together and make it work and find out that you have similar interests. For a relationship to work you need to be interested in the same things. I don't believe that you should have two totally different lifestyles or go separate ways every day. At some point, that is likely to become lonely.

At some point, if you are not able to build with the person that you love, then it would seem as though that that's not the person that's good for your soul and for your soul purpose. The person that's good for your soul purpose will fit and align directly to what you're called to do on this earth beyond finances. So to make sure that we covered everything, one of the things that you have to understand is that you are responsible for the people that you have around you. You're responsible for selecting the people that you date and understanding why they are compatible with you. Now, everybody you meet will not be compatible with you even if they are a nice person or a good vibe.

Everybody that you're interested in will not be compatible with your soul. Everybody that's compatible with you is not purposeful for you. You have to be able to begin to determine who's purposeful for your soul, who's compatible with your soul purpose, and who is good for your heart and mental health.

Love should build us, feed us, and help us develop even when we're whole. The love that we get into and share, even as a whole person, should still feed our soul, develop our mind, and encourage us to evolve beyond where we are.

Remember, the goal is to connect with someone, grow together, and learn more about each other, building something valuable and purposeful together. For this to work, you need to know how love feels to you.

What does it feel like for you to be loved? Do you believe you've ever felt genuine love? What is the love that you imagine and deserve? What kind of love would allow you to be your completely vulnerable self? You have to be accountable for setting your intentions and not settling until you understand what that love requires. That may require more time for self-reflection and introspection, allowing you to learn and understand yourself better. Time outside of the dating world helps you make choices that are good for you, not just for your image, the people around you, or your expectations. No Matter who you're with, if you carry a blessing in your life, God will bring things into your life as you go down almost any path, regardless of whether you're supposed to be with that person or not.

The goal is to ensure that you are selecting what you need, not what you want. Because when you select and understand what you need, that becomes your want. The more that you understand yourself, the more that you understand the past selections that you've made in mates, friends, business, and even where you spend your money; it will help you understand how to make better selections, commitments, and choices in whom you involve yourself.

Journal Thoughts

What exactly do you understand about the selections and choices of whom you've dated? Is there a commonality?

What do those choices in dating tell you about yourself?

You may be able to identify what may have seemed like depression, anxiety, or other types of mental illness. Consider the effects of mental illness based on the people that you've dated and the trauma that has them in survival mode. Oftentimes, whatever they are dealing with will also affect you, even if they don't discuss it.

When you begin to look at those selections and understand your own choices, then you will be able to see how you would like to move forward differently.

Section 3: Give Yourself Grace

You have to start forgiving yourself and acknowledging what you didn't previously know about yourself. Within faith and love, there are many things that you must become accountable for within yourself, including self-forgiveness and acknowledging who you are based on what you've learned through these books, the courses you've taken, and the lessons you've applied to your life so far.

The things you've learned from your own patterns will be the most monumental aspects of your evolution, growth, and maturity level elevation. First things first, there are aspects of who you are that contribute to your identity but have nothing to do with your own decisions as an adult, teenager, or at a level where you had control. It is very important that you make peace with the things that may have been influenced, caused, or a byproduct of something else beyond yourself.

Consider the environment, perhaps the guardianship or lack thereof, or the family you were born into, including the genetics you inherited from your parental units. There are some aspects of yourself that you have to learn to accept. You can't blame anybody for some things that you've experienced.

Just because it wasn't your fault, it doesn't mean that it was necessarily somebody else's fault. It may have been based on the circumstances that were present at the time. That was just the situation you so happened to be in; however, I want you to look at it a little bit deeper because whoever we are is based on who God created us to be. Every situation we face is based on the sole purpose of our lives, and everything is designed to help us grow and develop.

Not every person has to go through a difficult time to grow or become the best version of themselves.

However, without the proper guidance, it is more likely that you will endure some things that the proper guidance would've shielded you from bumping your head to learn. We believe that mistakes serve as lessons that turn misfortunes into blessings as we learn and grow. Acknowledge every beginning that you can recall of every feeling that you have. If you have an awkward feeling or a feeling that identifies a barrier that you want to heal, you first have to acknowledge where the barrier came from.

Insecurity may come from some neglect or abuse or some type of situation that didn't build you up to your highest capacity. As we grow, you may also realize that people will stifle your growth based on their comfort level. So, if someone was told they couldn't do something, then they might tell you that you can't do it too because someone said to them that.

It's important that you accept and acknowledge, even without an apology sometimes, the ramifications that some people's parents may have from being raised a certain way. When our parents became parents, they parented the best way they knew how. That is not to make an excuse for the things that your parents may or may not have done.

It's to help you gain understanding and clarity on how you and your parents may have ended up in those particular places. For many people up until this point, it has been easier to avoid, run, and band-aid the issues and emotions within that make them feel vulnerable. If they're bottling up or stifling their own ability to feel, heal, adjust, and cope with life differently, then naturally, they will instruct you based on what they apply to their own life.

It's just like a person that judges you, they're probably judging themselves even worse for the things that you don't know that they do or are involved in. The reason why they judge you is because they've judged themselves. The reason most people judge themselves is that they've been judged before.

Acknowledging where you came from will help you understand your perspective on love, the barriers that have been created in your attempts to love and be loved, and how to overcome those barriers. It will also help you heal from the experiences you've lived through. Acknowledging what you desire by acknowledging where you need to grow is essential for you to be the best you can be.

Let's reframe the idea that we love ourselves to be loved by someone else. Let's begin to focus on faith and love so that we can be the best versions of ourselves. It is vital for you to love yourself before you can want someone else to love you because you cannot allow someone to love you until you love and accept yourself. You won't be able to properly love, help, and encourage others or accept them if you have problems loving, encouraging, and accepting yourself.

When you acknowledge the areas where you need to grow, you're also acknowledging the things you desire. Once you've looked at all the men or women that you've been with, you should see your dating patterns based on what you've experienced. You will also learn how you like to be loved.

Based on what you've experienced, how have you allowed yourself to be loved? Thinking about what you want now and moving forward to the life that you want to build, what adjustments should be made about how you've allowed yourself to be loved, how you've loved yourself, and what you desire.

Fill in the blanks of things that have worked. What made you feel loved beyond sexual and instant gratification? What was emotionally supportive? When reflecting on your past relationships, pay attention to the things that were encouraging to your soul and helpful to your growth, as well as those that were toxic. Consider identifying your patterns in life, love, and faith, and then learn how to change them so that you can achieve the life, love, and faith you desire.

Ultimately, it's about finding areas that you want to grow in. Start by submitting to what you believe is your purpose, which is also beneficial for your soul, mind, and body. When you submit to what's healthy for you mentally, spiritually, financially, and physically, then you will be able to submit to someone who honors what's healthy for you.

When in a relationship, submission is not one-sided. The woman doesn't just submit to the man, the man also submits to the woman just as much as she submits to him. That's how they become connected and vulnerable to each other, allowing them to communicate openly and have freedom within the relationship. Once you begin to honor the different qualities about yourself, you allow someone who celebrates their differences and prioritizes their spiritual life and purpose over money. You often attract where you are at in life.

If you've been low before, as you elevate mentally, spiritually, financially, and physically, you will also view people differently, make different choices, refrain from judging, and embrace and allow people into your life in a more open and accepting way. You will also reject people that are not meant to be in your life. Please don't allow yourself to feel bad about things, people, places, events, or whatever it is that you let go of to honor your highest self.

When you attract what's best for you, you will attract people who honor what's best for you, too. When you begin to attract people that honor what's best for you, you will realize they also honor what's best for them. If the things you both honor connect and align, then what's best for each other will help you grow together and intertwine.

Growth is the key to attracting what you need, so identify, and remove all blockages and cultivate growth in those areas. If you feel triggered when someone does something, says something, or acts in a certain way, then those triggers are signaling that healing can still occur. Where there is healing to take place, there is growth to be had.

The evolution and growth will help you be the best version of yourself and attract everything and everybody that you need for where you're going. The law of attraction teaches that if you become it by thinking about it, then you will attract it. Are you attracting what's good for you with the way you think, talk, and behave? You may not stop attracting people who can identify with who you were before you decided to grow and heal. It's not really about who you attract as much as it's about who you entertain because you can attract anybody, but who you entertain will tell you where your life is going and what you really want for yourself.

Identify the areas where you need to grow. As you identify those areas, you will see your life begin to progress in those areas. You may cut off and meet new people, but the focus is growing the areas that you know you need to work on.

If you know you have an attitude, work on ways to improve it and control how you express yourself. If you know you have a spending or shopping problem, work on ways to gain self-control with spending. Remember that you are the only person that can help you grow.

Nobody can grow for you or force you to grow. You have to want growth. With growth comes change, and with change comes the application of what you know, which is wisdom. Wisdom helps you recognize the changes you need to make to become what you desire. Who you become is who you will entertain. Again, you may attract something that you're not, but what you entertain will tell me how much you've grown.

If you used to attract drug dealers, people who lie or steal, and you begin to adjust your life away from those things; you won't be around the same places to attract the same type of people. Even in those environments, when you know what's good for your soul, you will only entertain the people that are good for your soul.

There are certain things in life that you are meant to experience, and there are people in life who are meant to be a part of your path. Your job as CEO of your life is to identify who is assigned to your path and who is trying to attach themselves to your path as a leech. Learning to acknowledge things and being accountable is a crucial part of forgiving yourself, as we often suppress thoughts, behaviors, gifts, talents, and everything else related to love and our core identity. If we suppress those things that are at our core rather than understanding them, we can't fully love ourselves.

We have to be able to accept every single aspect of who we are. If not, then you don't fully accept yourself. If you don't fully accept yourself, then how in the world can anybody else accept you? How in the world could you fully love yourself and be the best version of yourself if you're not fully accepting and embracing yourself? The good, the bad, and the ugly. It's possible that some things people told you not to do were because they made them uncomfortable or were related to something they were personally dealing with. Don't let that make you reject who you are. Remember, you can always work to be better in areas that you aren't happy with. The person God created you to need every single portion of everything that's within you to be the best version of you. Forgive yourself for selecting and being accepting of things that you know you were better than.

You also need to understand and forgive yourself for the things you can't change. Life circumstances have molded you because God allowed those situations to help you become everything that you were designed to be in this lifetime. So when you begin to recognize your patterns and what you want to change, you will be able to understand the things that you can forgive about yourself that you can't change.

You can't change some of the things that happen to you or the experiences you've had, but you can definitely find and grow from the lessons from it all. Wisdom is about applying it to your life and seeing your life develop in a way that allows you to love yourself more and accept love as it comes.

Let's be realistic; just because somebody says they love you doesn't mean you should ignore how you are treated and accept it because they used the "L" word. Love is an action-based word, so telling someone that you love them is not enough. How do you show and express that love to that person in a way that they can receive it? How they receive love should determine how you give love.

Everyone doesn't receive love the same way. Some people may want gifts, and some may not, so you have to connect with your significant other, business partner(s), friends, and all of the people you choose to have around you to examine how they feel love. Then, you can make sure that you're loving them properly. In exchange, you must ensure that you can clearly explain how you want to be loved so that you can receive adequate love.

You deserve the love that you give and then some. Don't limit your love; love people who love you as authentically as you love them. You deserve a love that you don't have to be convinced of or beg for.

It's okay to love everybody because we're all human, and we have no reason not to love another human unless personally wronged. However, that does not mean you accept love that is not soul-nurturing.

You should have groundbreaking, soul-shaking love at your disposal. It should first come from within, but that love that comes from within should extend to all of your relationships. Then, you will be able to identify others who love themselves enough to also extend that love to you. This is where you find your support system, one that is not comprised of relatives. This is a community where you can both help and be helped and then develop to grow within it. Everyone needs the same support that they give. The goal of this love, curated by faith, also cultivates honor, support, respect, and encouragement. This kind of Love provides fullness from the love that you give and receive, as it's cultivated by faith, mindset, the people you are around, the things you do, and the places you go. All of those things matter, even when it comes to forgiving yourself and acknowledging stuff you've recently learned about yourself to apply them to your life. You may learn some things that may change the way you move around, the way you look at life, the way you act. What you learn from your experiences about yourself will change the places you go, the people you meet, and how you interact. However, do not change yourself to be accepted or liked by others; instead, evolve for your purpose and benefit.

I don't want you to lose sight of who you are and what your sole purpose is in nature, understanding, or the premise that I can only be accepted if I become what other people want me to be. You need to accept who you are. If people can't love you for who you are in your rawest, purest, most genuine form, then those aren't the people for you.

Please don't force yourself on people, and don't allow people to force themselves on you. Some people will say, "You have to love me, or you have to let me love you." This, in most cases, can be unhealthy, although a small few will attempt to love you when your trauma pushes them away genuinely. Identifying what you desire will help you avoid unhealthy situations because you will leave what doesn't serve a purpose.

We don't want you to continue in any unhealthy relationships. Anything toxic has to go. The more you love and accept yourself, the less you'll allow and accept those who do not love you wholeheartedly as a mate or friend, although you might be acquaintances. Just because a person isn't your best friend doesn't mean they are cool or fun to be around sometimes.

The primary goal of understanding this book is to recognize that the love you have within is the love you should keep around you and within your grasp. How you see yourself is reflected in your choices. What thoughts, behaviors, gifts, experiences, and talents could block love for you? What barriers have kept you from being loving or from receiving love? Being loving is just as important as receiving love because you can receive all the love in the world, but if you don't know how to return it, then the love you receive may diminish if it doesn't feel reciprocated. The only love that we want to diminish is toxic love.

For the love that you receive to increase, you have to let go of everything that doesn't allow love into your heart. If you had a hurt when you were 15 and you can't get over it, you need to revisit the scenario, the experience, and the circumstance that you were in that made you shy away from love. Figure out what part you played, what part other people played, and what lessons you can learn from the situation.

The ultimate mindset I encourage clients to adopt is never to experience the same thing twice, especially if they didn't achieve the desired result the first time. If you receive a negative outcome, you need to figure out in your mind how to change your narrative by finding a different way to achieve the desired result.

You should not hold on to anything from when you were 15, especially if you're above 30 or 25, for that matter. Learn how to feel things so that you can heal. Once you heal, you can let it go and grow; then, you can usher in new experiences to create new memories. The goal is to create memories to replace every bad experience that you've ever had. The catch is that you cannot replace bad experiences if you avoid facing them. Facing your past allows you the opportunity to see the lessons that help you heal and really grow.

All of this helps you to become what you desire and what you request from others.

Honestly, it would be unfair for you to want all these things, such as a house, car, trips, not to work, and excellent credit, and then bring nothing to the table. It's challenging to want someone to be spiritually sound, mentally healthy, and physically fit when they are inconsistent. You have to be willing to become what you desire to have as much as what you desire to attract.

When you become what you desire to have, you open yourself to receiving it. There are some things that you may have to open your mind to that may not make it to you. It may be beneficial for you to open your mind to receive the friends you're called to have with an understanding of the people around you.

You don't have to open your mind up to everything, especially anything that you're uncomfortable with. Avoid getting into anything that you wouldn't normally do, especially to win people over. What are the patterns in dating that you find within yourself? Do you have a type when you're dating? Do you see patterns or similarities in the kind of people you date? Do you see patterns in the relationships and friendships that you have? Do you see patterns? What are the patterns in your business affairs? Your patterns are likely to reflect one another and will reveal a great deal about your choices, decisions, and outcomes.

You will be able to understand who you are as a person and the things you've experienced based on your patterns in dating, building relationships, and navigating life. What would you change about yourself? No complaints. Focus only on growth. If there were things that you could grow within, what would those things be? Identify within yourself the areas that you could be more forgiving to yourself with past experiences, results, decisions, how you chose, and who you chose to be with or around.

Begin visiting all the places again that evoke a sense of something within you. Begin to see where you've been unforgiving and get an understanding of why you don't forgive. Make peace within yourself, and then make peace with those around you so that you can become the best version of what God created you to be on this earth.

Journal Thoughts

What areas don't you forgive yourself in?

What are you least accepting about yourself?

What can you do to accept and embrace yourself more?

What can you do to forgive yourself more?

What areas are you hardest on yourself about and why?

What patterns would you change if you could change the course of your life?

*Please answer the questions within the section in your journal workbook.

Section 4: Vulnerability

Give yourself permission to feel your emotions fully; do not run away from them. Listen, the most important thing you can do is to begin to feel what affects you. Everything in your body is God ordained with purpose.

Your emotions are sensors. If something is wrong, it is normal to sense that with your emotions. Many people will tell you not to believe everything you feel or think and not to get carried away with your emotions. This can be true, but you need to be able to acknowledge and process your emotions mentally, spiritually, and physically at times so that you can heal what you feel.

What emotions do you suppress, and how does that affect your ability to love? If you are upset and don't express how something has upset you, over time, it can create a barrier that may lead to anger and further upset. When you acknowledge and process your emotions, it helps you understand yourself better, especially if you tend to shut off your feelings. When you shut off your emotions, it creates a pressure point. If you continue to build up that pressure point, eventually, you'll explode. That emotion will overtake you, rather than you being able to control it and learn how to deal with it effectively.

When you notice that something is a trigger, it is essential to understand why you emotionally respond in that way. If something triggers jealousy, what about it sparks your jealousy? When you figure out what makes you jealous, try to trace the origins of your jealousy. Why do I feel jealous about this particular situation? What do you feel you deserve but lack? Thinking about the problem itself, understanding what circumstances you're facing today that made you feel that way, whether it's jealousy, envy, or hate.

If you're happy or sad, understand what in particular about the current situation makes you feel excited, mad, loved, appreciated, angry, depressed, or lonely. Listen to yourself and process what you feel. When you begin to feel an emotional way, you have to figure out in each situation what makes you feel that way. This is not only about negative triggers but any emotion you feel. Being aware of all your emotional highs and lows helps you shape your life and create more positive experiences than negative ones. Thinking back over the course of your life, have you always felt the way you feel now about things? If not, what happened to change you? What can you learn from it?

When you understand what's causing your feelings, you'll be able to understand what to heal and what to nourish. It's about gaining a deeper understanding of every previous situation, especially those with negative triggers. In unhealthy relationships, the connection will begin to evoke feelings not meant to be experienced by you because that type of relationship with that type of person in that place wasn't meant for you.

Sometimes, we find ourselves in situations with people, in places, and with things that we're not supposed to be involved with. Those experiences begin to be an emotional trigger. Every time you go through something similar to something that wasn't supposed to happen, that hurt you or made you feel bad. Even a smell can be associated with an experience and trigger an emotion. There are many types of triggers: lust, love, hate, fear, and pain.

Your job is to understand what things make you afraid and why. Dissect it. When did you first notice feeling that way? Because most of the things that we feel and are triggered by aren't the way we were as a child.

Nobody's born with triggers. Unless the mom was sad and depressed during the pregnancy, babies aren't born feeling sad. Life experiences made us experience each of these emotions.

Although this section is geared towards helping you regulate your emotions and understand the emotions you feel, if you need therapy, please consult a Licensed Therapist or a certified life coach who is accepting clients. All of our books advise that if you need medical attention, please seek the help of licensed medical professionals. If you are experiencing an emergency, please visit your nearest Hospital for the care you need. If you need coaching to navigate these challenges, then that's where I would come into play, or one of our other coaches.

If destructive emotions continue to resurface, it is essential to understand their origin and the reasons they recur so readily. You may even need to gain some clarity on why, from your perspective, another person would advise you not to feel and to suppress things. If you avoid the trigger, then one day, you're going to be triggered, and it will explode.

It will likely be more than you can handle, and you will feel overwhelmed. If you begin to understand instead of avoiding your triggers, then they will eventually be less traumatic.

They won't have the same effect on you as you begin to address why you feel that way when you feel triggered. Express yourself to yourself. You have to be able to talk to and understand yourself, then talk to God as you talk to yourself so that you can get those things off of your chest.

You don't always need someone else to talk to. Sometimes, you need to spend more time alone so that you can understand yourself better and learn to express yourself effectively. As you grow, mature, and enter into relationships, you will need to be able to express yourself effectively with others. When you enter a relationship, you cannot shut down because something triggers a response.

I mean, you can shut down, but it won't be healthy for the relationship. Learn how to spot triggers and embrace the fact that you're triggered.

If you're having a conversation or an experience with your partner, let them know that you feel triggered. Don't lash out at them or allow it to become a hindrance in your relationships, businesses, or other partnerships. You need to be able to communicate openly with everyone in your immediate circle. To communicate effectively with others, you have to be able to understand and express yourself clearly.

You can do this with a journal, a notebook, or take notes on your phone. There are different ways for you to get those things out and for you to hear yourself talk about what's wrong.

There's nothing wrong with encouraging yourself. There's nothing wrong with getting expert advice about your life from the expert of your life, which is you. Take those things into prayer. Prayer is talking to God (The Universe) in a way that allows you to express yourself, your desires, wants, and needs. This also opens you to hearing back from God (The Universe). However, God (The Universe) decides to speak with you.

When you experience an emotion, truly feel it, walk through it, and understand why you feel the way you do. Understand the trigger, how it affects you, and why. If you begin to cry, ask yourself, "Why am I crying about this?" What is it about this that's hurting me so deeply that it makes me want to cry?"

Sometimes, a triggered emotion goes back to abandonment, neglect, or a different form of abuse. It may be verbal, mental, or financial abuse. Various things happen throughout our lives, and not all abuse is physical or obvious.

We are all raised differently, educated differently, and we all experience things in different ways. This means our perspectives, mindsets, understanding, and the way we deal with things are different.
It's beneficial for you to be able to acknowledge your emotions, process them

mentally, and gain an understanding of why you feel that way. If you need to seek therapy to help you understand why you feel a certain way, whether it's grief, remorse, guilt, joy, peace, happiness, or depression. Whatever that feeling is — good or bad — you need to be able to understand both.

Too often, the bad feelings are what we focus on the most because, usually, when we feel bad, it affects everything and everybody around us. You also need to understand what triggers your happiness. What brings you joy? What makes you laugh? What gives you peace? And what makes you feel loved? All of these things are important when entering a relationship and cultivating love based on faith.

As you decipher your emotions, you will understand what makes you happy, who you are naturally, and what is added to you by the circumstances and the people around you. As you grow and experience new things, you'll apply your new ways of thinking and your new perspective based on your healing.

Your desire to heal brings more circumstances and situations that will assist in your growth. Your limits will be tested, and when they are, you will see your growth. You'll feel good about yourself when you start responding differently than you have in the past.

When you enter a relationship with a significant other or a business partner or become close-knit friends or family, your healing will be essential for growth. The ability to grow through new experiences while learning from past experiences reshapes your mind and becomes wisdom.

Your healing forms a whole new existence of being through your thinking and living. As new love enters your life, be expressive and embracing because new love will bring new feelings of connection.

New love after healing does not mean that there will not be some things you have to grow through or learn within the new relationship to exceed everything that you've ever experienced. New relationships after healing can still carry some residual hurt that you must endure because people are imperfect, and life is unpredictable. Although it's impossible to avoid hurt, that does not mean that those close to you should be hurting you on purpose.

There is a certain amount of a learning curve that you will endure in learning to love a new person. You have to give room for that person to get to know you and for the mistakes that may occur during the process of learning, growing, and falling in love for the first time. As long as you both understand that you are there because of love, not the benefits, then accepting the growth that comes with learning about your relationships will help you flourish.

Learn to love the right people, but be aware of red flags and signs that indicate someone may not be right for you. This isn't based on a look because a person can look amazing, say all the right things, and be as eloquent as you think a good person should be, but if their heart isn't right, they have to be able to tell the difference. Whether someone's heart is right or not could be based on their inability to address the things they need to heal from.

Carrying around unhealed pain in your heart and the inability to express things can't always be seen. Some hearts can be carriers of every bad thing that has ever happened, yet they smile and appear giddy towards others. Think about Robin Williams, the comedian and actor, he unalived himself while being known to help others smile and looking out for those living in poverty.

How a person handles situations reveals where their heart is at. How they view life, interact with others, or whether they judge people. All of these things will begin to reveal a person's character and the type of perspective they have. How do they reciprocate the love that you have for yourself that's shared with them? The goal is love minus the ego. When you mix love, faith, and hope, you begin to unlock new dimensions of yourself and the world around you.

The question is, how do you deal with your emotions? What are five things that aggravate or irritate you that you have not gotten over? Are there emotions that you run from or shut down when you feel? Because you need to be able to process every single emotion to understand and accept yourself. When you get angry, it's okay to be angry as long as you don't act out of anger. It's OK to be sad as long as you don't act out of sadness.

Depression is acceptable as long as you don't stay depressed and act out of depression. If you find yourself feeling sad, first identify the reason behind your sadness and then incorporate activities that address the underlying cause. Figure out ways to change that sadness into gratitude. If you are depressed because you lost a loved one, think about the lessons that you've learned from that loved one that you can carry with you and implement into your daily life. This will help you feel closer to that person and facilitate the grief process.

Journal Thoughts

How can you help other people with your healing?

How can you help people who are like the ones you lost?

How do you manage your emotions?

What are five things that aggravate or irritate you that you have not gotten over?

Are there emotions that you run from or shut down when you feel?

It's about changing the narrative within yourself first so that you can then begin to change the narrative of those around you. The things that you've gone through, the emotions that you feel, they're there to help you. Once you've enabled yourself with understanding yourself, loving yourself, and embracing yourself, those things will help you to help others.

Section 5: The Blessing in Lessons

Embrace the fact that your greatest blessing will often come from a difficult lesson. I want you to understand that everything that you've ever endured in life is a lesson waiting to be learned. Whether it is a good thing, a bad thing, or something indifferent you endured.

Every experience holds a significant blessing that's disguised as a lesson. First, understand what makes an experience a lesson. You must understand that every single thing you have ever endured is for your growth. Take time to reflect on it to identify areas where you can either grow or make a slight adjustment.

There is always room for improvement in one aspect or another. It may be your attitude, mindset, train of thought, or reactionary behavior patterns. Consider things a little bit differently, but in each experience, it's okay.

When considering the good aspects of this experience, what made it a positive experience, and how can I create more experiences like this? Figure out what made the experience good but challenging. What thing did you have to overcome? What things did you face? What shaped it into a good experience? When evaluating a good experience, you still need to consider whether any negative events occurred during the process of achieving it.

Some good experiences may not be entirely positive; sometimes, trouble, trauma, or healing may occur, but the result is ultimately beneficial, kind of like seeing the light at the end of the tunnel. Your goal with each positive experience is to identify the pros and cons, weighing the benefits against the drawbacks. See which challenges you had to overcome so that you can know what challenges you may face moving forward that lead to more good experiences.

When dealing with negative experiences, the focus for most people is on the negative and what caused it; however, within that negative experience lies a valuable lesson to be learned. You have the opportunity to determine what contributed to that being a negative experience.

With both positive and negative experiences, you have to take full accountability and responsibility for every role in the experience. Some experiences may not be solely based on yourself or things that you can control.

Accountability will be key, but that doesn't mean you were at fault; it simply means taking responsibility for everything that happened. If you experience something negative, what are five contributing positive factors? What were the five contributing negative factors? You need to attribute specific accountability to the things you contributed to the experience, whether it was through your mindset, actions, responses, thinking patterns, a learned experience, or if you aligned with what was already happening. Then, you also need to figure out who else played a role in both your positive and negative experiences.

Remember to keep track of the types of people you have around when you have positive experiences and who is around during negative experiences as well. You need to determine what kinds of mindsets and people contribute to your negative and positive experiences. Don't blame any negative thing that you've experienced solely on someone else. There is accountability within yourself unless you were a small child, held at gunpoint, or forced by abuse to do something. Otherwise, there is a responsibility and accountability that you can take for any negative experience.

How did you contribute to that negative experience? If it was a relationship, what part did you play in making the relationship more difficult? This doesn't always mean you did something "wrong." Even if you start changing yourself in a relationship to make it work, you may consider it a negative experience because it has long-term effects.

You may become unsure of yourself, second-guessing everything, and that can be a negative experience that carries over into your next relationship.

Those accountability factors will either make you or break you for your next relationship. Based on your past relationships, you can decide that you don't want to re-experience something or that you want to have the experience while monitoring how things unfold along the way.

Take accountability by acknowledging you did A, B, C, and D to contribute to this good, bad, or indifferent situation. Then, consider revisiting E, F, and G to adjust the aspects of your behavior that contributed to the last experience. Think about it. In a relationship, are you fussy? Do you nag? Do you demand your way? Are you seeking control? Are you too giving? Will you break yourself down so that others can build themselves up? Are you taken away from your creativity? Are you letting your creativity flourish?

When you're dealing with a job or a negative business experience, do you approach it with an open mind? Did you contribute to solution-based information to get a good result? Was there anything you could have done to change the circumstances? What would you change to create a different result?

With each positive experience and each negative or challenging experience, you will always strive to find the lesson. The lessons are within the truth that you face in yourself. When you look into a mirror and reflect on each different experience, you should gain a new insight into yourself. You should learn new ways to deal with things.

You should begin to learn the patterns of success, failure, and being stagnant. Being stagnant is an indifferent scenario where you have both good and bad experiences, as well as experiences that fall somewhere in between. An indifferent experience can be received either positively or negatively.

How can indifferent things be made into a positive experience? How can an indifferent experience that leaves you feeling unfulfilled be transformed for the better? In each one of these lesson-based blessings that come from experiences, you may only have one experience, one time in your life, but you may be faced with other experiences that have the same or similar narrative.

Being prepared for anything that you may face, regardless of the narrative, is based on seeing how something that you endured before helps you get to a better result now. The goal for you is to determine what you can learn from each of your experiences, including your childhood, adolescence, and young adult years. If you were in your twenties, what aspects of your adolescent and teenage years have you taken from and decided to use, adjust, and apply to where you're going in your twenties?

Within your twenties, they should be your years of experimentation. Don't experiment with wild drugs or anything that would take control of your body or have you out of your right mind ultimately. You don't have to experiment with a sex trade industry or anything that would remove you from your purpose within God.

If God guides you to an area, then, by all means, venture down that area. But the moment that you realize that what you're doing is no longer purposeful, it's okay to stop, reassess, and come back to more purposeful things. As you get to your twenties, it is good for you to figure yourself out.

When you're a small child, an adolescent, and a teenager, you have not figured yourself out yet. Your actions are dictated by either your parents, school, or some other authority that's controlling what you do, say, and who you hang around. You need to base your twenties on the desires of your own heart, to learn yourself, to understand yourself, to accept and love yourself.
You don't have to rush to get married if you're not already married. Figure out what

you like first before trying to change someone into who you like. Don't be in a rush to have multiple sex partners if you have not already had numerous sex partners. Don't let anyone pressure you into anything. Being a virgin, celibate, and practicing abstinence is brilliant and a safety precaution.

Your most significant lessons in your twenties will lead you to the biggest blessings of your thirties. For most people, the 30s (the thirties) is when life begins to come together, and everything you've gone through makes sense when weighed against where you are now.

That's when you've experienced enough to figure out what you really want to do for the rest of your life, where you begin to set up your plans for retirement or leading into retirement. If you are in your twenties, go party. Have a drink if you're able to maintain and control your alcohol limits, but drink responsibly.

Have your first experience when you're ready. If you've already had your first sexual experience, grow from it before you have your next sexual experience. The way you love yourself dictates the type of person that you entertain.

Let me be honest with you.

Sometimes, we may love ourselves and attract someone who does not love themselves enough to love us the way we love ourselves. That's okay as long as you're not expecting more from them than you can actually get. The next lesson will come from healing.

As you reflect on your adolescence and childhood, you may discover that there are some things you need to heal from. There may be parental neglect, fights, attitude, or temper problems that you may have.

There may be certain things that you learn to survive as an adolescent that can influence who you become as a teenager. When you become a teenager, of course, life gets a little bit more difficult because you have a little bit more leeway to do what you want to do. You have a little bit more control over yourself.

However, in those times, we still need to take the time to figure out the world around us as we navigate it. The lessons that you will find in your healing will be the lessons that you will use when you get to your mid-20s and 30s. The more you work on yourself earlier on, the less likely you will have experiences later on that are from destructive behavior patterns.

If you were without a parent, whether death or just being absent, causing any neglect or abandonment issues in your 20s, you can heal from that. You can begin to figure out what made you feel neglected or abandoned. When you are grieving a deceased parent, you have to look at what they stood for and taught you and find ways to dedicate a portion of your purpose to them. Find ways to honor yourself that will make you feel better and more seen. Who do you think you would've been if the situation was the way you wished? Then, live that out.

Most people who deal with neglect or abandonment issues feel like they don't matter. It's important to find ways within yourself to emphasize how much you matter in this world. Find ways within yourself to improve your self-esteem, acknowledging the positive aspects of your childhood and adolescence years. This allows you to see how everything has shaped you into the person you are today and who you decide to become tomorrow.

Some may not be able to heal everything on their own; they may need to seek medical assistance from a therapist or a psychiatrist to get medicine that helps manage emotions. There is definitely a need to address the issues that you know are unresolved or unhealed from your past.

The lessons you gain from healing will help you understand the type of people you begin to love beyond yourself. The more you love yourself, the more you will require people to love you as much as you love yourself, or they won't be able to have access to you. If you learn to love yourself more, you will become less willing to accept love that does not feel genuine.

There are different types of love. Some love to make you feel loved in a way that resonates within your soul. Then there is the surface-level love that sounds good but has no substance behind it. The love that humans innately desire is love with substance. Deeper self-love prompts you to reevaluate your friendships and romantic relationships, including those with a boyfriend or girlfriend.

It may take you some time to figure out which friends are genuinely genuine and which ones are there for their own benefit.

Sometimes, our childhood trauma is not caused by our parents. Sometimes, we are hurt by the people we call friends or desire to be friends with or by those placed within our surroundings with whom we have no choice but to befriend.

If you live in an area, you are more likely to be friends with the people that you live close to based solely on proximity. It may be a gang that you can't avoid or a religious community you feel pressured to join.

When you love yourself more, you will be better able to distinguish between good friends and those who are not so good and create a more effective support system. Different friends will take you down different paths, and the company you keep greatly influences the heights you reach and the way you think. Knowing this can change everything.

Some friends and people will be around when good things happen. And then there are people you will find around when not-so-good things happen.

Don't try to change people, but change the people you surround yourself with. Not everyone will accompany you throughout your entire life journey. There are people you've known for 10, 15, or 20 years who may not have as good intentions as somebody you may have met two or three months ago. A key point is identifying who is intentionally aligned with your mindset, goals, and what you want to achieve purposefully in the world.

Your purposeful alignment will take you the furthest in life. Those that align with your purpose are those that are supposed to be in your life for longer seasons. Be reminded that there are people in your life for a reason, for a season, and for a lifetime.

The things that happen in your experience with each person you encounter will tell you what type of person you are dealing with. You will know if they're supposed to be around for a long time or if they're only supposed to be around for a little while. Some people will build with you over time, and you will realize they will be around for a lifetime. Grace can be given during difficult times in life, but always trust a person's behavior patterns.

As you discover and uncover different lessons within each experience you've learned up until now, you will begin to see signs of things from the past, whether good, bad, or indifferent. This is the way to start understanding where you are, where you're going, and what you're meant to be.

Signs are not just red flags to get out of there. Signs are also caution signs of something to be aware of and green flags that indicate someone is safe.

For example, if a person is a liar, you need to be aware of that. That's a caution sign that they could lie to you. Once you see what type of lies they tell, if you stay around that long, you'll know if they lie about small or big things. One thing is sure: if they are a liar, then lies will be told. Over time, if you deal with many liars, you will pick up on signs of a liar.

What are the signs and the things that you have picked up about people based on your experiences? Your experiences will teach you what to look out for. Some things you will already know as soon as you see specific behavior patterns indicate what is to come.

There are signs of abuse, of good-natured, good-hearted people, and of people who manipulate your mind, want your money, and the benefits of being around you. All kinds of signs are available to those with a mind to see. Seeing and recognizing the signs starts with accountability for what we see and who we have around us to help us understand the signs God is trying to provide.

God provides signs in every instance of life and every manner. The Book "Spiritual Human Behavior" discusses the various signs of God and how God communicates in more detail. Signs are from God and all around you.

Think about seeing a red bird or a butterfly whenever you think about a topic or an Idea. Would that become a sign for you?

Sometimes, we get goosebumps on our arms as a sign from within; other times, we feel something in the pit of our stomach that tells us something is wrong. The goal is to utilize your experiences, the knowledge you've gained in or out of school, and the insights you've gained through conversation. Your knowledge and experiences will provide you with your most valuable lessons, as they can be used to shape future experiences.

Your experiences will determine the things you desire to learn about. Getting knowledge and applying it is the true sign of wisdom. What lessons do you learn from the signs that God has given you? What signs have you learned from the lessons of your healing? You are responsible for making sure that you begin to recognize the things that God is showing you, placing them in front of you, and all of what God has for you.

This book explores faith and love, but the most profound love is self-love. When you exude the self-love necessary to learn and receive blessings within experiences, you will begin to exude love and see signs and lessons in every situation. Learning this will help you pause and reflect on the signs God is giving you when making decisions. What signs do I need to ask for? What direction am I going? And what has me going in this direction? The goal overall is never to make the same error twice.

It's an error because if you didn't like the result, your job is to identify the lesson and determine how you obtained the result you didn't like. What could you do differently? What could you change? What aspect of thinking could you alter to get what God has for you? All these things will take you into a different place of love within yourself, your life, your surroundings, and your environment. You will begin cultivating the love you seek by cultivating healing and lessons from within. The more you heal and learn from within, the more those things will reflect around you.

The lessons you learn will serve as your foundation for everything you do. Don't let yourself be controlled by the past or things outside your control. However, be more proactive in everything we do moving forward.

Being proactive means not waiting until something happens and then trying to figure out how it happened. It means preparing for anything you want to do or your goal beforehand. Mental preparation ensures that when the opportunity presents itself, success happens. What is the opportunity that you're waiting for?

Your preparation depends on your goals and what's already been accomplished. Within all of that, you will see your lessons of love and resilience. You will see how those things you've been through prepared you for your next level and blessing to come.

All of your lessons become your personal love Bible. Take notes on what you learn about yourself from your experiences, what things to watch for, what things to avoid, what things to try, what things to accept, and what not to accept. The more you learn those things, the more lessons of love you can apply to your life and in your relationships with others.

Cultivating love the way you need it comes from figuring out every lesson you could have learned from mentors, teachers, instructors, good jobs, bad jobs, bad bosses, and good bosses. Some things will teach you, encourage you, prove you, and try you throughout everything you do. Everything is a lesson.

Completing and publishing this book for you is a lesson. Writing, going back to edit the book, fixing things that were okay in the original audiobook but not okay in the paperback book—that's a lesson because some books don't edit out anything. Observing the difference through market research and personal enjoyment of literature offers valuable lessons.

Precision versus whatever comes out. The goal is to make precise decisions in every instance so that each lesson can bring a blessing. The blessing is already there; you have to have a mind that sees it. Every step closer to your heart's desire is a win.

No matter the outcome of an experience, good, bad, or indifferent. The blessing is in the lesson of preparation for similar encounters. You can grow from everything you've been through and apply the signs of patterned behaviors and commonalities to life to get the desired results.
Suppose you're wondering how this works for love when setting your intentions for healthy relationships and family building. In that case, It is because having healthy relationships requires inner work on yourself to prevent hurting innocent people based on past trauma.

You have to work on healing yourself on the deepest level. Sometimes, these lessons aren't learned before entering a relationship;

healthy relationships can trigger some healing. Good relationships can help you identify areas where you may be toxic if you are open to acknowledging the truth about yourself.

Lessons don't always come from bad. Lessons don't always come from indifference. Sometimes, lessons can also be learned from positive experiences. It's equally important to understand the value of positive experiences. You should figure out what made those experiences positive to create more positive experiences. When you have a negative experience, identify what aspects made it negative, and use that knowledge to create a more positive experience by learning from those negative traits. Everybody has some negative aspects to work on; some toxic issues manifest in relationships.

In each of those situations, you may not always realize that you're toxic and consider the negative things you've contributed to a relationship. But take the time to review, reflect, and reconsider. You will see both the negative and positive aspects that contributed to relationships, where you could have handled things differently, looked at things differently, or approached them differently. Then, you will begin to understand how people may have triggered that experience.

Consider how other people may have brought negativity to you when you may not have been negative in the initial stages. It's your job to be accountable and responsible for your actions in relationships, the people in those relationships, and the contributions they make that you may overlook.

There are lessons that you won't know you need until something triggers them. Identify them as lessons and not hard times. Think of it as a stern test; what kind of test taker are you? Studying is required, so examine your life and see what you can learn from your past decisions and the uncontrollable circumstances that have shaped them.

If you're going through something difficult, look for the lesson. If you're going through something positive, look for the lesson. As you customize your life based on your results, create the mindset of a tailored life.

There is a lesson in everything you do: to be more consistent and precise, communicate more effectively, take better notes, think things through differently, or change how you apply things to your life. Within the lessons of life, you will find your greatest blessing in disguise.

Journal Thoughts

What lessons have you learned from evaluating the things that you've experienced in life?

What lessons can you take from negative relationships that you've had so that you can become accountable to the part that you played in that negative relationship?

What things were contributed by others in those negative relationships?

Section 6: The Evolution of Growth.

When considering growth and its evolution, consider changing what doesn't work based on what you've already tried.

Section 5 briefly discusses accountability, highlighting the positive aspects of each experience and scenario and then identifies the negatives in each scenario. It also addressed the roles you played in various aspects of your life and the roles others played so that you can understand what works and what doesn't. This section will encourage you to consider how growth evolves each person to new depths.

As you make adjustments to curate the life and lifestyle you desire, you should apply the things you've learned. The things that you would go back to change in certain situations, where you may have a little regret or want to do it differently. Start to see it as a test coming to evaluate your next win.

Every time you didn't get the desired result in the past, technically, you didn't achieve elevation. If you apply the lessons, you will likely avoid similar situations in the future.

If you cycle through boyfriends, jobs, friendships, or trauma, you need to consider what you would have done differently to change the outcome in the last circumstance. The things that you would do differently to change that outcome will begin to shape your current reality and manifest the things that you want to see.

Shaping your life helps you align your life with those who are meant to be in it and with your purpose. To track the evolution of your goals, create a timeline outlining how you plan to accomplish them. If you continue to accumulate debt, have credit issues, or fall behind on your bills, the goal is to determine how much time you need to get this under control. Once you get that under control, when faced with something similar, you'll have a different response, which also creates a different result. That different result could be the next step in developing healthier habits and behavior patterns.

How much time do you need in between relationships to get to know yourself again, recalibrate, and balance out who you are after the relationships that you've been through? How would you change the narrative of the past relationships to progress in the future?

This is where accountability comes in. If, in the past, you were a nagger, cheater, complainer, or didn't bring enough to the table, figure out how to be less of a cheater, nagger, or liar and how to bring more to the table. When you begin to examine things from that narrative, it will prompt you to grow, as you should no longer settle for the same result.

You must take initiative in what you do, with whom you speak, and with whom you surround yourself. Planning changes the course of your reality, allowing you to avoid repeating the same experiences. Most goals should have about three or four scales of goal milestones. This includes short-term goals (six months to one year), medium-term goals (two to three years), and long-term goals (five years).

If you are a super planner and strategically working to reach goals like love in your life, whether it's with self-love or just exercising your faith based on the goals you are setting forth. Consider having a seven to 10-year goal plan.

The most important factor in goal setting is always being open to God, if you are a believer, and exercising your faith while trusting God in the process. Being willing to change, stop, halt, shift, or completely dismiss whatever goals you have set. Leave room for God to fill in the gap within your purpose or change how things unfold. We have a plan based on what we know now, what we see now, what we think now, and what we are currently.

There is a larger plan that supersedes our thinking, aligning with the purpose of your particular path. The things you see based on who and where you are and the path you see in front of you are what get you in the direction of purposeful alignment. The more you continue to align with your purpose and the closer you get to that path, the narrower the path becomes due to the things, people, and mindsets you will let go of to continue along the path of purpose.

In addition, understand how your goal list is documented and how to take those steps. Move with purpose, and cultivate a life you love. Purpose is fueled by moving forward in faith.

Give yourself a timeframe to invest in the things that you find purposeful. You can give yourself a timeframe for relationships, a job, a career, or a study path. You can give yourself time for business, structure it as you prefer, and set the goals you want to achieve in both business and relationships.

Personally, I allow up to five years for any relationship or business to work. That does not mean that if I'm not a millionaire in five years, my pursuit will stop. If I haven't made progressive steps toward reaching the goals I've set, then some changes need to occur so that I can stay purposeful and aligned with my goals moving forward.

If it has not worked within three to five years, then some things need to be changed to get closer to the desired advancement. This method can be applied to relationships, as well as business, personal, spiritual, mental, and physical goals. It allows enough time for a shift to occur and determine if it's working or not. If you stop something too quickly, you may miss something that could have been a minor adjustment to keep things going.

If you consistently go long enough, you'll see progression. Progression is meeting midterm goals and seeing provision along the way.

The progression is marked by progress as you achieve goals and continue to set higher ones. Now, as you begin to climb those goals, you will be tested. You will have to exercise your faith.

Based on your plans, the things you've considered, and how you've weighed the potential challenges ahead, you can move forward with greater strength. Knowing that you're either reaching milestones and making headway as you move forward or identifying areas that need adjustment to get to where you're supposed to go. When something needs to be adjusted along the way, you make minor changes, noting when things work and when they don't. Even if you don't change it immediately, if you notice something is working, you should note that it is working. Knowing that it will work, you can proceed to implement that into your life.

However, you also need to note when things don't work so that when it's time to make adjustments, you can ensure you reach your five-year goal. For instance, if you have a five-year goal, consider making adjustments every two and a half years to stay on track.

You could make adjustments every year to ensure you're making the best adjustments when necessary. If no adjustments are needed, then don't make it for the sake of making adjustments. If what you're doing is working, then Work What Works.

Understanding what works for you may not work for somebody else. The things that are faith for you may not be faith for somebody else.

Life is customized for you in particular. Goals are based on the result you would like to reach, have, accomplish, and manifest in that timeframe. As you make adjustments, you'll see the progression of your goals, and it'll seem more manageable, but that's not because it's becoming easier. You're just becoming better.

When you begin to assess love on your journey in your faith, it's a different kind of faith. Many things should not be manipulated.

Let's talk about manifesting. If you're not in a relationship, you may want to manifest one. If you're in a relationship, you may want to manifest a better one; if you've already manifested a great one, you may want to move on to the next step.

It's beneficial to have relationship goals and to incorporate your faith into your relationship, but you should avoid using faith to manipulate your relationship. Read that again.

It is beneficial to incorporate faith into your relationship, but you should not use it to manipulate your partner.

It's very easy to say what God said. It's very easy to tell people that you love them based on how God loves them, but nothing is better proof of how you feel than showing how you feel. Daily patterns through actions speaks louder than words.

People can manipulate using love based on words, gaslighting, or using perceived faith. There are many types and forms of manipulation when it comes to faith and love. Primarily because people want to be in love, and sometimes they'll settle for what looks like love, even if the love is not there.

If love is not there and you settle for it, then you're settling for what you weren't getting instead of getting what you need. Be sure not to use faith to manipulate love or to evaluate the love being received. Faith-based love is different.

You cannot manipulate it. You have to go off of what is shown. You should not attempt to force love.

You can't even force love to benefit your faith. Love is an understanding, a pause of consideration, communication, a conversation.

Love is a connection.

Faith-based love is not based on what you can say. Love is the wings on a caterpillar that makes it a butterfly in its natural process of evolution. Faith is just the caterpillar. Faith is inching by with no persistent determination.

Love takes "caterpillar" faith and gives it wings. It allows you to do whatever God is guiding you into with the speed and grace of a butterfly. It's easy to walk in faith, but when you add love to faith, that's what elevates your ability to embrace, accept, be, grow in, and balance the love amongst it all.

In addition to exercising your faith and reaching your goals, when you cultivate love within yourself, you'll begin to see the world with compassion, which enables you to empathize and help others achieve their goals as you pursue yours. Love will calibrate you; faith will align you, and you will be able to get where you're trying to go without manipulation. Faith should not be used as the sole "method" for achieving by simply saying you have faith.

You must align your actions with your thoughts and your thoughts with your behavior, producing results based on what you're trusting God for while acknowledging your current situation. As you flow into alignment, the things that used to be challenging for someone not aligned or prepared or that aren't purposeful become easy. When a person is in alignment, they handle pressure differently than someone who is not aligned. They won't be able to do the same things that the person with a purpose for that can do. That's "Grace" associated directly with your purpose and soul calling.

When you flow in alignment with your purpose, your difficulties become easy. Count the Cost of your plan. Prepare, Prepare, Prepare!

It is crucial to understand what you're getting yourself into when setting goals, regardless of the type of goal you're setting. You must understand what it will take to reach your goals, whether it's love, career, or any other objective. All of these things begin to affect your ability to have a relationship and the type of relationship you're going to have, especially if it's going to be based on faith.

Be prepared for lessons to be applied daily as you calibrate and start making adjustments. As you remove all the barriers that you find within that keep you from loving, lessons from your past become the key to loving someone differently. This is based on the areas where you need to improve and adjust within yourself, enabling you to love yourself more effectively. As a result, you can receive the love you need and give the love that is required from you as well.

As you learn lessons and apply them, the test becomes more evident and more straightforward as you exercise your ability to reason with the understanding of what led to your previous results. You'll be able to recognize when you are tested with something similar, then adjust your approach by saying, "I'm going to approach this differently this time and see what outcome I get." And I am going to think the plan so far out that I know the possibilities of all the outcomes that could come if I do this or that if this or that changes, or if that's narrative or this is the narrative."

The goal is to be so on point in the spiritual process of being aligned in love that the difficulties, bumps in the road, hiccups, or anything that comes as you master faith cultivated by love because of all the things you already consider. It becomes and looks easy to others because you're flowing in it. As you align with your purpose, the more you will have confidence in the path God is leading you on, and the evolution of your growth becomes evident.

Take as much time as you need to assess new methods. Listen, don't think that everything will be perfect in six months, but it will be better than when you first started the journey.

Things might not be perfect in a year, but you will have grown towards perfection. Although some people may have a quicker process, others may not, and you should not be discouraged.

It may take time for you to achieve the things that God has in store for you. As you move forward, you must make the necessary adjustments to remain aligned with your purpose and achieve the goals you have set, all while being open to God's love so that you can receive all the blessings God has in store for you.

There is provision and grace in your path that comes along with what you're doing. The more growth you experience, the more you apply the things you already know, and the more the alignment flows.

The alignment that flows can be defined as being able to take the path and everything that comes with it without being discouraged under pressure, even when pressure or the potential for discouragement is present. You will be able to move along the alignment of that path so well that it flows like water under a bridge, seamless, like a river or a lake. You don't see it moving at the top. Still, there's definitely some movement going on within the water.

Journal Thoughts

What areas could you see yourself growing in?

What goals would you like to set?

How far in advance would you like to set those goals so that you can see the evolution of your growth in each step and every process?

If you are already working on and achieving your goals, what things work for you and what don't you so that you can make the proper adjustments to achieve the results you want?

As long as you continue to make adjustments based on your heart's desires, you will always have them fulfilled.

Section 7: Building a Faith Community

Let's talk about soul connections and the feeling of being part of a faithful tribe.

Now that you've gone through all sections of all four books answered all the questions, and completed all your interwork, hopefully, you've reached a point where you feel ready to connect and attract the people meant to be in your life.

This can come in different forms. When considering soul connections and soulmates, it's essential to recognize that these connections and soulmates are not limited to romantic relationships.

Again, soul connections and soulmates are not limited to romantic relationships.

You may have a soul connection or a soulmate that is your best friend, your sister, your brother, your mother, your father, your husband, your grandmother, your grandfather, or your wife. The soul connection is the way your purpose within God intertwines perfectly with another soul's connection with God.

Those two souls begin to connect purposefully and create something very Godly. The relationship is founded on a deep connection of the soul, a shared purpose, as well as open and effective communication. When discussing soul connections and faithful tribes, it's far more than just romance.

Many people automatically try to make soulmates only about sexual partners. Even when considering soul ties, it does not necessarily have to do anything with a sexual relationship, although sex can influence a soul tie. You can become entangled with another person's soul by being consumed by their day-to-day drama, including gossip, listening to someone else's problems, and tuning in to the wrong things. If you become too engulfed, your life can either begin to mimic that person's life, where you start to take on the drama of their life, or you can become lost in it.

That is another form of a soul tie. Most people consider soul ties to be a sexual exchange where once you have sex with a person, now your souls are intertwined. Your souls intertwine way before sex if you have a soul tie. Soul ties are unhealthy connections, often with someone you may have had a strong emotional attachment to in the past.

You could enter into a soul connection with someone that is only for a reason. This means that God (The Universe) sent them into your life at this particular place in this particular time for this reason, and only for this specific reason did this person enter into your life.

If you extend that beyond the parameter set, then that relationship can become less favorable. It can become perverted when it exceeds the parameters for which it was intended to operate and lead to dysfunction if it takes away from your life.

When you talk about reason and then season, you may meet someone who is destined to be in your life, where you play a part in their life, and they play a part in yours for a set time known as a season. Seasons on the spiritual and faith side are not like the four seasons that we experience in nature.

You may have someone that God places in your life to help you with that healing. Once the healing is over, that person may no longer be a part of your life. Once that healing is over, your position with that person, your relationship, and your connection with them are now also over. Most connections are a result of the stage of life you're in.

Help is available for growing seasons, healing seasons, and grieving seasons. A place, a pattern, an experience, or a mindset can all determine seasons. There are people whom God, the universe, and all nature align to help you overcome your season. There will be people that God will align on your path in each season for a particular reason.

Some people are destined to be in your life for a lifetime. They may not be everything that you need them to be at that time.

They may need to do some work, just as you do. They may or may not be healed. If you're healed, you may have something that can contribute to what their mission, purpose, and lifestyle are heading, and they may have something for you. As you come together, the relationship builds a lifetime connection within the soul. Some relationships are meant to last a lifetime.

Suppose you are unaware of the lifetime connection potential and the lifetime connection space. In that case, you may get shuffled into the wrong connection, thinking that it's a lifetime when it's actually a season or that it's a reason when it's supposed to be a lifetime. If you do that, you will have many things out of place and need to be redirected to get you back to the connections you need.

Some connections, once they're lost, are lost forever.

Some connections are supposed to be rekindled, becoming those that are meant to last a lifetime. Nine times out of 10, the people assigned to you go the distance and don't become attachments to your plans.

An attachment is somebody who tries to hold on to what's going on because they see it's happening and it's going strong, and they're just trying to attach to it. The people that are assigned to you are those people whose purpose aligns with you. The people will be the ones who help you as you help them simultaneously reach the goals that have been set forth.

Now that you understand the inner you, you can attract people who are good for you because you carry yourself differently. You're in different places based on the goals you have, your new mindset, and your newfound understanding of who you are rather than what others want you to be. You walk into a room and stop wondering if everybody likes you, wondering if you're dressed to standard.

The opinions of others begin to become mute because now you are reassured within your purpose and on purposeful alignment so that you know that you're on your assignment with no attachments. As align with your purposeful assignment on this alignment, now those people that are supposed to align with you can be drawn into you. Ensure that only the intended attendees are present to ensure there is room for everyone.

As you see the changes, know that you have made adjustments to yourself, as this is the goal you set. Not that you're changing things about yourself to reach goals; you are adjusting the things around you based on who you're realizing that you truly are. Once you know who you truly are, your personality traits, your patterns, how you think, why you think how you think, what helped form those patterns, what patterns you need to change, and what patterns are healthy, once you've healed the toxicity of what you were raised in, then you can begin to draw people and attract people and converse with people that are just as healed and whole and healthy as you are, mentally, spiritually, emotionally.

Discussing attracting people who are financially where you are often comes down the line because sometimes you may meet a person who is in a financial struggle, but in their mind, they consider themselves wise. In their thoughts, they're progressive. In their spirit, they are ascending towards the things of God, but they've hit a financially difficult time. You may be able to help them in areas of learning about finances while they're able to help you in ways of attaining a purposeful future.
Learn yourself so well that you begin to pick, choose, and align with those who know themselves just as well and are as accepting of themselves as you are of yourself.

The people who will help you carry out your purpose, see your vision, and walk with you on your mission are those who understand the purpose, faith, love, and connections.

They know what it means to stand 10 toes down, flat-footed as a foundation for where you're going together. To be faithful to your growth is to be faithful to the type of relationships that you build.

Be faithful to the type of friendships that you establish and the people that you associate with day to day because some people are good for you. Some people will not bring you your best results because they're not a lifetime assignment to your purpose. They are an attachment to your past and the traumas that you've had, and they're trying to hold on to that moment when you're trying to grow from that.

That's how you grow away from people because there are people who will hold on to where you came from to stay connected. However, the people who are supposed to be there will be fully developed and ready to go.

They will be purposefully minded, have goals aligned with yours, and already be working towards the things that connect you. When you do come together, when the universe does align, it will be the perfect situation to grow, build, love, connect, and become a tribe together.

The faithful tribe is those who are with you and accountable, responsible, willing to correct you, willing to hold you, willing to care for you, with you, and willing to help you heal because nobody can heal you but you unless you need a third party with you to assist you in healing. You have to teach yourself how to treat yourself so that you can learn how to set the standards you need to meet the expectations you desire.

Once you understand yourself and make the necessary adjustments, you'll know the type of people you need in your life. That might start with creating a list.

Not a list for a boyfriend or necessarily for a potential mate. This book intends to promote healthy, loving, and family relationships.

Teach yourself what would be healthy for you based on your mental, spiritual health, physical health, and emotional health because you don't want to be in a relationship, a friendship, or an association with someone that's not good for your mental health. It doesn't matter how purposeful it seems if it's bothering your mental, spiritual, or emotional health to the point where you think that something is wrong with you. It's time to reevaluate if that's a purposeful connection. That soul tribe will help you align more closely with your purpose based on your unique vibe. As you structure your life around your goals, focusing on the outcomes you desire for the future, you will begin to establish the standards you need to achieve for your goals and dreams to come true.

You must set the tone for the standards and expectations of those within the parameters of that family tribe. Don't put people in a contract with you so that they can maintain the type of relationship you're into. You need to align with people who are naturally good for you, not those who have to change who they are to be with you or minimize who they are to be with you. Nor should you be around people that you have to minimize yourself for so that you can be around them.

What you want to do is attract people who, if nobody is around, are truly themselves.

This is who they're when people are or aren't watching, whether they're talking to God or not. It's good to know where people come from when you meet them in church or any other religious setting where they have suppressed their natural state to please a leader or others. You have to figure out who that person was before they got saved, joined a religion, got involved in whatever they're into, and changed who they were naturally.

If anything changes or disrupts their relationship with that religion, sect, or environment, they will likely revert to their previous state of mind. So we're not looking for or connecting with just anybody.

We're allowing people to be everything they were born to be naturally so that we can connect with the right people instead of forcing them to be who they're not. It prevents connecting with people who are not who they claim to be, just for the sake of a connection, which turns out to be a valuable lesson, ultimately a blessing. If you can connect with those who are purposeful for you, then that blessing does not have to come from a negative lesson.

It can come from experiencing growth. There are lessons to be learned from experiencing growth, as well as from facing a negative experience or something that requires correction. Just going along the path of God will teach you a lesson within itself because, within that path, you will learn so much about yourself, your faith, your spirituality, and your walk and connection with God.

Those things form the connection that you have with your soul's purposeful base, the connections that are meant to last a lifetime.

You have to accept who God gives you as they will align with your purpose and life plan. And anybody who does not align with your purpose and the life plan that God has assigned you, you have to let them go.

It may seem crazy, like you just can't cut people off, but snip, snip. Sometimes, you have to dip, dip.

If you allow people to hold on to you, that's an attachment; eventually, those attachments can become corrupted and cause harm. If those attachments become corrupted and cause viruses, then you're left to find a detour to get back in sync with those with whom you're supposed to be connected.

Ensure that anything that doesn't align with God's purpose for you comes to a graceful end. Learn how to move away from it and allow God to reveal who is for you and who is not so that you can part ways peacefully. Go on, be happy in your life with a deep understanding of faith.

It's essential that as you cultivate healthy relationships that are beneficial for your mental, spiritual, and emotional well-being and that are also purposeful, you will start to experience happiness. You'll see the difference in who you are as an individual and how you come together to build things around the world that will help make the world a better place.

Journal Thoughts

As you finish this book, what do you need in your tribe to reach your purpose?

What vibes would align with the purpose that God gave you individually?

If you are married, how can you connect with other married and/or single individuals who share your purpose?

Both married and single people have a place in this world.

Single and married people can coexist and find a place in the world together as long as it's established on respect, support, boundaries, love, peace, and unity. And this is not a ploy for you to begin having affairs or anything like that.

However, there are some things that single people need to do within their purpose that married people may not be able to do, shouldn't do, or that could be unhealthy for their marriage if they hadn't found someone soulfully connected to their purpose. Don't ostracize singles or get married for the wrong reasons. Healthy connections within your soul tribe should be so strong, confident, and trusting that everyone can all come together and accomplish greater things in unity than could be done separately.

Thank you for your purchase. Please check out our
other books.

Spiritual Human Behavior
Faith 101
Faith 201
Faith 301
The Unknown Power
It's My Time

www.ingramcontent.com/pod-product-compliance
Lightning Source LLC
Chambersburg PA
CBHW070147080526
44586CB00015B/1875